Poems of Mine

Gene Fowler Jr

BookLeaf Publishing
India | USA | UK

Made with ❤ on the BookLeaf Publishing Platform
www.bookleafpub.in
www.bookleafpub.com

To all my friends who offered encouragement over the years, I thank you! To my niece Brittany who sent me this challenge—thank you! To my facebook friends Julieann Painter, Margie Pulliam, and Holly Foshag, thank you for your encouragement & inspiration. To my two wonderful sisters, Joy Keffer, & Patricia Smith, thank you so much for always being there for me, and for your support above & beyond! I love you both dearly! Last but certainly not least, thank you Mom for all that you do for me & for everything you have always done! I love you so much!

Preface

Hello readers, I hope you enjoy reading my book of poems. Some of them offer advice, such as it may be. Others represent a fantasy of meeting some of my favorite songwriters and lyricists. Some are political, so if you like trump, you'd probably be better served to skip those, or if you're not afraid of learning the truth, read them with an open mind. You just might learn something. The Midas Touch Network tells the truth, good, bad, or indifferent. You can believe what they tell you. Several of the poems are about my deceased nephew Dallas, who departed this world on September 7, 2018 at the age of 22.

This book came about because my niece sent me a link to a poetry contest, which I entered with backing from my little sister Trish Smith, and big sis Joy Keffer. Thank you both again for all the love and support you have afforded me. Some of these poems are just for pure entertainment. They were fun to write, and I hope you have fun reading them. A few were also inspired by everyday life.

One poem in particular is very special to me. I went to visit a buddy in Chillicothe, Ohio. While I was there, I met a really nice woman, who happened to be homeless, not due to any fault of her own. I stopped on my way home at a roadside rest area just north of Gallipolis, and wrote "The Procrastinating Prodigal" in February 2023. I hope you enjoy reading my book of poems.

TABLE OF CONTENTS

The Procrastinating Prodigal (X2)

The Procrastinating Prodigal,
Seems to never get anything done.
Do you need someone responsible?
He's definitely not the one.
There's only one thing Steve's good at—
He really knows how to have fun.
It would not surprise me one bit,
If I saw him smoking a blunt!
Steve has unruly long, grey hair,
He's always been an old hippy.
He has never tolerated,
Anyone who's getting lippy.
The way he goes and wanders around,
You might think Steve was a gypsy.
There have been a few occasions,
I've seen him a little tipsy!

I heard that once upon a time,
Steve asked his boss for some time off
At what he was wanting to do,
Many people would surely scoff!
You know Steve, he pulled this thing off,
With his unusual aplomb.
He took his guitar to Europe,
Just so he could become a bum.
I happened upon his story,
By a simple twist of fate.
I'll watch or read anything,
If to John Prine it relates!
When this dude met John,
It was the most hilarious story.
I instantly became a fan,
Of Steve Poltz, Oh Boy!
He put me in mind of,
The Procrastinating Prodigal.
An alter-ego of mine,
Who's in no way mythological.
Steve is highly intelligent,
Do not focus on the *high*.
If he ever asked for directions,
You may bet he wasn't shy.
Watching his mannerisms,

& facial expressions,
Would lift anyone's spirit,
Out of the darkest depression.
Steve is genuine, the real deal,
He is a great entertainer.
I wonder how many lawyers,
Steve has on legal retainer?
If you ever get to see him;
Steve is now on my bucket list.
You won't be disappointed,
I can assure you of this!
It was truly miraculous,
Fate and blind luck led me to find,
The Procrastinating Prodigal,
I'd only imagined in my mind.
These little twists & turns of fate,
Are enhanced by fortuitous timing.
Some of the best events in life,
Occur then need redefining.
I don't have any idea if Steve,
When on tour, comes this far east.
Steve rolls with the flow, in his life,
Nothing phases him in the least.
Perhaps there will soon come a day,
When Steve and I will meet,

I will probably laugh so hard,
I might fall right out of my seat!

The Rainbow Bridge

There is a bridge somewhere out there,
Humans are not allowed to cross;
We would never, ever find it,
We'd manage to only get lost.
From everything that I've learned,
From all that I've ever been told—
humans are not the right species,
We do not have the proper soul.
It's those who are most pure of heart,
Who are allowed to cross this bridge.
To love unconditionally,
Is the toll that they have to give.
They are our faithful companions,
Throughout all of life's tempests.

They're a part of our family,
They surely are not just our pets!
You might be a person who loves cats,
Other folks might love only dogs.
It might possibly be your thing,
That your whole life you have loved frogs.
You may have now possibly guessed,
The bridge it is of which I speak;
It is always okay to cry,
Grieving doesn't mean you are weak!
Although we cannot cross this bridge,
It's by another route we arrive;
Yes, we will see our pets again,
Over there on the other side.

Come Back to Yourself

Come back to yourself,
No matter where you've been;
Come back to yourself,
You're buried deep within.
Buried in turmoil & chaos,
It's easy to become lost;
Come back to yourself,
You're more than worth the cost!

You keep yourself hidden,
Hid away like Fort Knox gold;
Come out & share with us,
A story you've never told.
Come back to yourself,
We don't care where you've been;

Come back & be yourself,
It's okay to start over again.

Why don't you come out?
To hear what I have to say;
Just thought I'd stop by,
To see if you'd come out to p[ay.
I don't see you coming,
I'll stop back by another day;
I wish you'd have come out,
Gotta smoke it 'fore it rots away.

So come back to yourself,
For so long you've been away;
Come back & enjoy life,
Smile when skies are grey.
Another day will dawn,
Perhaps a day just like today;
With sunshiny blue sky,
That gets you high in their own way.

It's never too late,
For a fresh start to begin;
To begin the life you want,
To be happy once again!

Ringo's feelin' the sunshine,
You can feel it too;
Let go of hate & embrace love,
It's such an easy thing to do!

Angels & Wings

I don't really know,
If angels have wings;
I do love to listen,
When I hear an angel sing;
The last one I heard,
Was several years ago,
Miss Alisson Krause,
At a Willie Nelson show!
What a beautiful voice,
So pure in every way;
"It Is Well" with my soul,
I get chills even today
Only her sweet voice,
So pleasing to my ear;
She sang it a capella,

Loud, strong, & clear.
It was truly Heavenly,
Over Willie's sound system;
If you've never heard Alisson live,
You don't know what you're missin'!
Alisson came back onstage,
To sing with Bonnie Raitte;
Not sure now what they sang,
I do remember it was great!
Two beautiful ladies,
Both are superstars;
Bonnie Raitte sure can play,
A bluesy slide guitar!
People came from miles around,
To be present on that day;
What a show it was,
There on the Walnut Creek Stage.
Another angel played first,
Miss Stephanie Quail;
A beautiful young lady,
Who had a beautiful voice as well.
Lukas Nelson played next,
With his band Promise of the Real;
He's Willie's son,
Any show he could steal.

Lukas is wildly talented,
He's down to earth, not uppity;
He plays guitar like Stevie Ray,
& dare I say it? Jimi!
Songwriting is a talent,
Lukas is superbly gifted;
Kris told him he's a songwriter,
No other option is to be permitted.
When Bonnie Raitte finished,
Her part of the show;
She told us all who were there,
There's a place I have to go;
I'm heading over to Nashville,
To see a dear old friend of mine;
Maybe you all have heard of him,
My friend's name is John Prine!
This announcement was greeted,
By a loud, resounding cheer;
Wish somehow John could've heard it,
I know it would've tickled his ear.
Then Willie Nelson came out,
The man we'd all come to see;
He opened with a song
About some river named Whiskey!
What a show we saw,

It didn't seem seven hours long;
Good music & good friends,
All joined together in song.
What a wonderful day!
Not one harsh word was spoken;
The entire ensemble joined in,
To end with *Will the Circle be Unbroken.*

True Love

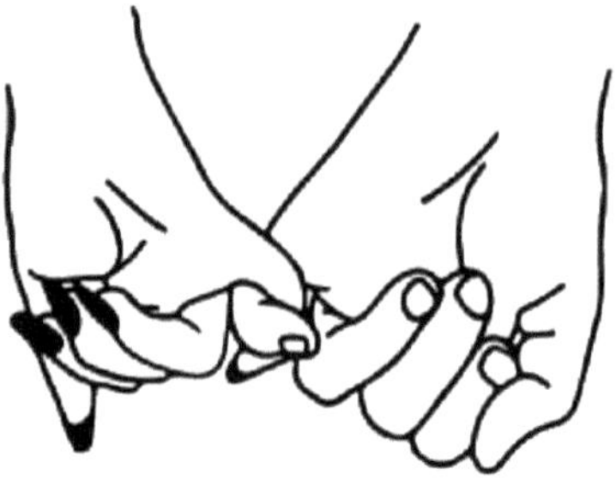

I'd walk ten miles,
Just to see your beautiful smile.
Each step I take brings me nearer,
As your beauty becomes increasingly clearer.
You are my Enchantress,
Your voluptuousness I long to caress,
No other woman can hold a candle,
You're so much more than they can handle.
Your beauty shines brighter than the
noon-day sun,
Your soul glistens like Andromeda One.
Our souls intertwine as we sojourn together,
All of creation is finer than fine in any
weather.
The day we met, my spirit soared to unbound
heights,

You also keep me grounded as we lay together each night.
You are my goddess in all ways immortal,
Perfection personified in no way abnormal.
Having breakfast with you, my bright morning star,
Beats the Hell out of sitting alone, drunk in some bar!
I'm drawn to you by your sensual magnetism,
Your worldviews unite us in liberal activism.
We could never be driven blindly by hatred,
Prejudice, bias, & bigotry can't coexist where love is created.
We lift each other up as if we're floating in a dream,
If love were a crop, yours would be the cream.
I stowed away in your aura... riding the rising tide,
It was a joyous, momentous day when you became my bride!
Nothing out there can stop us if we stick with God's plan,
Remaining meek & humble while being guided by the Almighty's hand.

Trusting in Him to lead us to a peaceful,
loving paradise,
I'm completely blessed, Babe, you are the
anchor of my life!
Joined together for all eternity, dancing &
singing each night,
You're the ultimate, perfect Lady for me, God
made you just right!
Some of the people who read this, might
believe it's all hype,
They'd quickly become addicted if our love
could be smoked in a pipe.
There will always be doubters who lack the
essence to be fully alive,
True love focuses you on your other, your
devotion to them is supersized!

Original Procrastinating Prodigal

He's the Procrastinating Prodigal,
He never gets anything done,
The only time he's never late,
Is when it's time to have some fun!
He sits around & smokes his pipe,
Wondering what's become of his life.
Seems that all his hopes & dreams,
Have flown away & faded from sight.

It's as if no one is aware,
Of so many people's plight,
There are so many things,
So many things that just aren't right.
People out in the street,

Living out in the cold,
I wonder how they're damaged,
Wonder what's wrong in their souls.
Surely these folks once had,
Ambitions, dreams, & goals,
It appears that life,
Has raked them over the coals.
They're down but not out,
They're out but not down,
Something's gotta give,
To turn this thing around.

When you lie down tonight,
To sleep in your comfortable bed,
Think about the people on the street,
Do you think they've even been fed?
Perhaps they found food in a dumpster,
Out there in the dead of night,
Maybe they think it's not that bad,
Like it's acceptable & almost alright.

What would you do,
If you had nowhere to go?
Would you be able to survive,
Out there in this cold?

Really, it's so sad,
Yet so commonplace,
So many homeless people,
So many have been displaced.
My, how the mighty have fallen,
Fallen far from grace,
Many people blame drugs,
I blame the human race!

We don't take care of our own,
We never have & never will,
We just don't want to pay,
Don't want to pay that bill.
A lot of the people up there,
Up there on Capitol Hill,
Have forgotten what it's like,
Forgotten how it feels.
How it feels to be cold & hungry,
If they've ever felt that way at all,
Who look down on the homeless
downtrodden,
See them as nothing more than animals.
A simple twist of fate,
Can turn your life on its head,
Human empathy & compassion,

Are traits either dying or dead!
What would it take for you,
To be forced to steal?
The look in your hungry child's eyes,
Would that make it real?
Being cold & hungry,
Are two things no one should feel,
The homeless in the U.S.A.,
Deserve a better deal!

Special

When you're special you can feel it,
Others can sense it too;
At times ideas come at you,
Right straight out of the blue!
We're not really special,
It's more like we are tools;
Whose tools for what purpose?
Sorry, I haven't a clue.
A Divine communication tool,
Used by the LORD above;
A tool used by drunken aliens,
Who should put the plug,
Back into the jug!
I'm asking for your thoughts,
Please take this under consideration;
Where do our thoughts come from?
From whence comes our inspiration?

I covet your opinion on this matter,
You are under no obligation;
I'd love to hear from you,
No matter your level of education..
Do we form our own thoughts?
Do we have unknown contributors?
When we have a good idea,
Is it from a thought-sender's competitor?
Are some thought-senders really drunk?
Did one get caught up in traffic?
Did one get cloned? That one girl needs to be boned!
From the thoughts I receive,
My sender's on permanent vacation,
No, I don't know what that means, can I get an explanation?
He likes to play games from checkers & dominoes,
To playing nude charades.
If you were to play these charades,
Would you make the grade?
Which could give new meaning to,
"Is it bigger than a bread box?"
You may find out a friend isn't a bonafide Goldilocks..

New Rule just in,
You're allowed to wear socks,
What's a bunch of loons called?
I don't know either but I've got a flock.
New Rule number two,
This one is a daisy;
If you're to be my friend,
You've got to be somewhat crazy!
Okay, where was I,
My thought-sender got distracted;
He may have seen something shiny,
Like 'coons & crows, to them he's attracted.
Maybe he threw me a curveball,
To change my direction;
When dealing with thought-senders,
It's always better to use discretion!

Maybe a better name for them,
Might be "thought-provoker"?
Wonder who had Stephen King?
Who had Bram Stoker?
Can you imagine,
Every thought that's ever been?
Do they drift off into space?

Circle back to be thought again?
What would it be like,
To read someone's thoughts?
Do you think they might sense you,
Think maybe you'd get caught?
What would you say,
In your own defense?
I was just checking to see,
Whether you have competence.
I've also been wondering,
Why are you always so content?
Yeah, that's right,
Are you really that ignorant?
Tell them they're the reason,
You are such a shitty friend!
I bet they'd tell you,
It's not me, it's you again
and again. .
You wouldn't have to ask,,
If they like you or not,
You'd know right away,
You'd know what's what!
Wouldn't that be special?
It would be in fact;
Lots of truths coming at you,

With no time to redact.

Truths are a thing of beauty,
The most desirous of all treasures;
If only truths & falsehoods,
Were meted out in equal measure.
Truths bring about knowledge,
With knowledge at times comes wisdom;
Common sense is left out,
Although at times it may drop in.
At times my thoughts run wild & free,
Like Mustangs out in Nevada;
Other times they encompass everything,
That's right, the whole enchilada!
My thought-provoker must've got sideways,
Seems I was just there myself the other day.
On the edge is a fine line,
On the edge things could go either way;
One side has the most beautiful view,
On the other side is a dark abyss;
The view comes with pain-free bliss,
Tormented souls fill the chasm so don't be
remiss.
Hope in itself is a wonderful thing,
Hope in Christ is perfect, without peer;

Hope in Christ brings serene contentment,
Hope in Christ comes without fear.
We all must decide our own destination,
It's something only you decide for yourself.
To spend eternity in euphoric nirvana,
Or spend it endlessly tormented in Hell.
For the gift of eternal life with Jesus,
Ask Him for forgiveness.
The very best we could ever do,
Would be totally meritless.

Missing Something

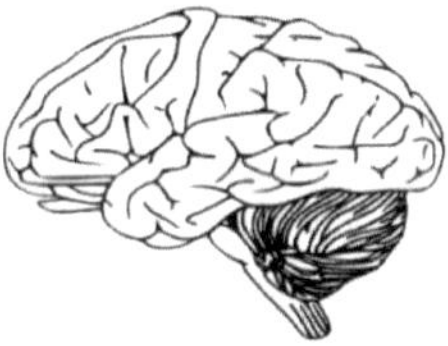

My mind paid me a visit,
It was just the other day;
It'd been gone so long,
I had forgotten it went away.
It just showed up,
Never said where it'd been;
I never thought to ask,
It'd been gone since I was ten.
I did ask how long,
It intended to stay;
It said that all depends,
We'll take it day by day.
You can't miss a thing,
A thing you've never had;
You can never be hep,
If you never know the fad.
This could be a good thing,

It could most certainly be bad;
We don't really need to know,
For that I am eternally glad!

Life is Fragile

Life is fragile,
Time is fleeting;
I'll say it again,
It's worth repeating.
Life is fragile,
Time is fleeting;
The Earth's resources,
Are rapidly depleting.
What will we do,
When we can't breathe the air?
What can we do?
Doesn't anyone care?

Life is so short,
Do we know what we're eating?
There are times when I wonder,

Is "Fuck You" a greeting?
Life is tender,
People can be callous;
Why should we care,
About the names that they call us?
I've met lots of folks,
There are some that deserve beating;
I just can't abide,
All the lying & cheating.
They claim it takes all kinds,
To make the world go around;
There are some who should be lost,
Be lost & never found.
I know there'd be some,
Some loved ones I'd miss;
There are so many out there,
That ain't worth a pint of piss!
I suppose I should try,
To be more tactful when speaking;
Can the others not see,
All the havoc they are wreaking?
Some are so bad,
Their own mothers are weeping;
They cannot be good,
Not even when they're sleeping.

Yes, life is fragile,
Time, it is racing;
I have a hard time finding,
All the things I'm misplacing.
Does this happen to you too?
As we add up the years?'
I just had it in my hand,
It has to be here!
I've no idea how this happens,
There is no rhyme nor reason;
Why things disappear,
Then come back in the reappearing season.

As time races on,
I don't mean to complain;
I just wish something could be done,
To ease the chronic pain.
I know it's out there,
Be it in chemicals or plants;
If only the powers that be,
Saw our pain as significant!
Being in chronic pain sucks,
Are we to just grin & bear it?
Hot tar & feathers,

There are some I'd see wear it.
I don't think they care,
It's always all about them;
If we'd only help each other,
The way that we were meant.
Life is so fragile,
Time is not compensating;
A world where we all helped each other,
Wouldn't that be a world worth creating?

Into the Light

Come out of the darkness,
Step into the light,
Let's all now join together,
It's past the time to unite.
The rich are getting richer,
While we're barely scraping by,
If things continue this way,
We won't be able to get high.
Gonna plant a seed tomorrow,
To guard against that day,
That day when Mr. Breeze,
Will have blown it all away.
We won't survive another cycle,
If shit keeps going this way,
Why wait until tomorrow,

Why not plant a seed today?

Yeah, the rich are getting richer,
At an accelerated pace,
They now own rocket ships,
To blast themselves into space!
While some are bumming dollars,
Others are bumming dimes,
I never thought I'd live to see,
Such sad & desperate times!
We've all turned against each other,
While they're flying oh so high,
The time has come for us to join together,
It's time to set things right!
No one gives a damn about us,
No one cares about our plight,
Why wait until tomorrow,
Why not plant a seed tonight?

The times are really hard now,
It will keep on getting worse,
So, plant yourself a garden,
Don't forget to grow some herbs.
The world is moving on now,
The transition's no longer slow,

So, plant a seed tomorrow,
Plant a seed & watch it grow.

Yeah, this world is getting shitty,
This world is turning dark,
No one cares about each other,
It's high damn time we start!
We're commanded to love each other,
So why is this so damned hard?
Is it that we'd have bombs,
With no one to bombard?

Step into the sunlight,
Leave your worries in the dark,
Looking out for one another,
Would be a tremendous start!
If we would help each other,
If we could somehow get along,
We could solve so many problems,
We could right a bunch of wrongs!
So, plant a seed tomorrow,
You can still plant a seed today,
Plant a seed of friendship,
Things don't have to be this way!

So, plant yourself a garden,
Grow yourself some weed,
Fuck all these corporations!
Fuck them & their greed!!

We can make it without them,
They'll not last long without us,
We'll be just fine & dandy!
While they return to dust!

So, plant love in your garden,
Weed out all the hate,
Plant love in your garden,
The hour is growing late.
We're all here to love each other,
This shall be our creed.
So, plant yourself a garden,
Grow everything you need!

Moved On

The world has moved on,
No one knows where it went,
No one has any cash,
All the paper money's been spent.
With no coin in circulation,
Society returned to the barter system,
If you have nothing to offer,
We may end your subscription.
Yeah, the world has moved along,
Ain't nobody around,
Your subscription is your life,
You could end up in the ground.

If your head is in the clouds,
You can't see what's on the ground,
Besides being a stuck-up snob,

You'll never say, "Look what I just found!"
I've lost several dear friends,
I wish were still around,
I do have many good memories,
If my mind remains somewhat sound.

This world went & left us,
Left us here on our own,
Not many things are better,
Than reaping what you've sown
That's if you've sown kindness,
Good deeds and good vibes.
Nothing good is returned,
If all you've sown is diatribe

The world took an exit,
Hit the exit ramp too fast.
Strange events can occur,
Slingshot you into the past.
If ever you get a do over,
Proceed with all caution.
What would an item from your life,
Bring if it were sold at auction?.

Mr. News

Hey! You there!
On my TV news;
I don't need your opinion,
I can form my own views!
Just tell me what's happened,
In the world today;
In the fewest words possible,
I like it that way.

I don't need your slant,
I don't want you to opine;
Just pass along the facts,
They don't even have to rhyme.
The reason is for me,
To figure out on my own;
Just give me the news,
Skip the dog & pony show!

Why would you think,
Your take matters to me?
I have two eyes,
I see what they see..
Good, honest news,
Is direct & to the point;
I can mull it all over,
While I'm smoking my joint.

You can keep your spin,
I'm both cognizant & aware;
Just lay out the facts,
What happened & where.
I don't need your opinion,
Don't need to know what you would do;
I can draw my own conclusions,
Just as easily as you do.

So go out there & get the story,
Turn in your report;
Don't try to shape my views,
You know that's a tort.
Deliver up your story,
Allow the facts to stand alone;
That's where your job ends,

So go give your dog a bone!

The Time is Now

The time has now come,
For these words to be spoken;
How much more garbage & trash,
Can we dump into our oceans?
It's really quite sickening,
All this garbage that we live in;
If we keep trashing the oceans,
We'll soon have no room to swim.
It really is disheartening,
To see wildlife become entangled;
All wrapped up in plastic,
The poor critters are being mangled!
It's all a sad reflection,
Of our human state;
Litterbugs should face large fines,
This is not open for debate.
We are the caretakers of this planet,

We've no other options to choose;
If we are left without clean air & water,
What else have we to lose?

The Great Unknown

What do we know,
About the great unknown?
Is Jesus up there watching us?
Sitting on His throne.
How many children die,
Before they are fully grown?
Do alien life-forms exist,
Or are we all alone?

What if we knew about,
This thing, the great unknown?
When we see what's there,
Will our minds be blown?
Will it be paradise,
A paradise of our very own?

These are things I ponder,
When I'm sitting around all alone.

What do you reckon is out there?
Out there beyond the sky;
Stars, planets, & galaxies?
Comets streaking by?
What is really out there?
Out in the great unknown;
Will we travel at light speed?
Have others already flown?
Will we simply teleport,
One place to another?
Only think you are at a place,
Then you're there, no bother.
To travel by merely thinking,
Not on roads with painted lines;
No other energy needed,
Only the power of your mind.

Will we have wings like angels?
Will we need them to fly?
Could we float & zip around?
If not, I wonder why.
Our souls are ever weightless,

We leave our bodies behind;
If somehow I could find out,
Without first having to die.

Thoughts

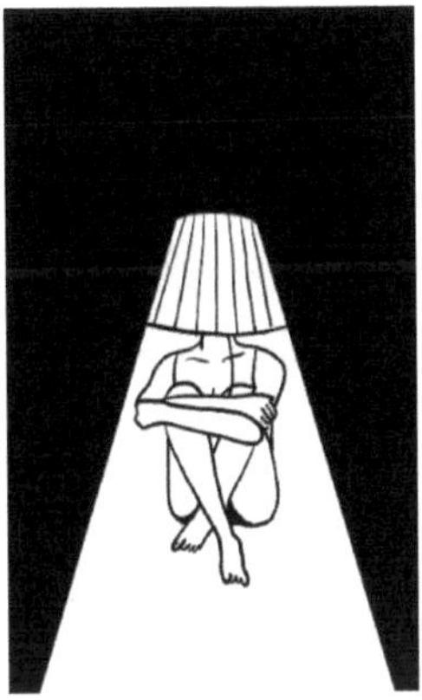

I've never been lucky at love,
Never been lucky at cards;
Never been much of a gambler,
Though I have found luck as a bard.
The words come from thoughts,
Where do the thoughts come from;
Sometimes out of thin air,
I write a line, the next just comes.
Are they from another dimension?
Do they arrive through a portal?
From beyond the farthest galaxies,
Hard to fathom by a mere mortal.
One line comes through clean,
The next line might arrive jumbled;

Putting them into sequence,
Keeps me truly humbled.
At times they arrive as incomplete thoughts,
It's them that are impossible to finish;
A wise man once said to set it aside,
It'll come back without a blemish.
Words can be fun, some have varying
meanings,
Did you ever read a book you've already read?
Ever been questioned only to be interrogated?
Ever said again, something you'd already said?
Words fascinate me, some words hold power,
Some describe people, places, or occurrence,
How you feel or what you think,
Tell about your day, or a sinister act
abhorrent.
When the lines flow fluid & sequential,
A magical thing takes place;
Complete, sequential phrases are divine,
Tend to put a smile on my face,
Broken thoughts arrive a total mess,
Needing a lot of work, as *mess* suggests,
That's usually when I walk away,
When I set it aside & give it a rest.
From disordered chaos,

To some form of coherence,
A phenomenon so hard to explain,
I don't have the words or endurance.

Pursued By Demons

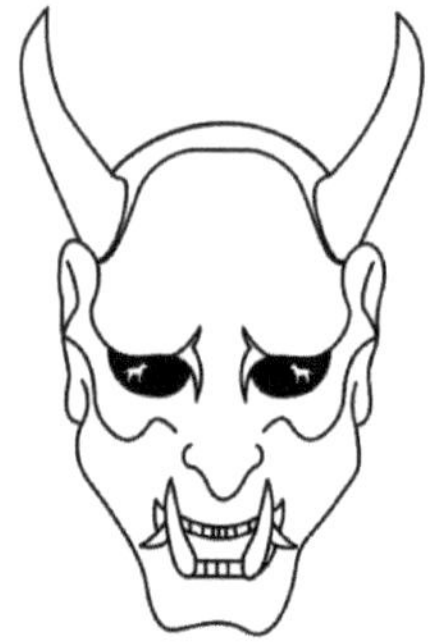

Being pursued by demons,
While searching for angels,
Being hindered & harassed,
Knowing not what the road foretells.
Nothing in life comes easy,
This I know all too well,
LORD, please cast my demons,
Back into the pits of Hell.
Once they almost had me,
Somehow I slipped away,
They never even knew I left,
May not realize it to this day.
When they discover I escaped,
For me they will come searching,
None of us can ever know,
Around which corner they'll be lurking.

They'll want to even the score,
I know this fact for certain,
If they only knew when they find me,
It's them that'll be hurting.
My all-p[owerful Lord & Savior,
He is constantly by my side,
Once Jesus Christ gets after them,
They'll have no place to hide.
Whenever that day dawns,
For them, I may feel pity,
They're no longer welcome here,
In my Father's golden city.
They were banished long ago,
Many ages & eons have since passed,
When they chose to follow Lucifer,
Their deaths & fate had been cast.
Whenever we choose evil,
Evil unto us is returned,
We always reap what we sow,
This lesson needs to be learned.
Do not be afraid of them,
When out they come to seek you,
My LORD & Savior saved my soul,
Jesus Christ will save yours too!

The Critique By the Creek

We held a critique down by the creek,
I tell ya, man, things were looking bleak.
That's when Jeannie appeared, asking,
“What is it you seek?”
I tried to remain calm, trying hard not to
freak.
Right then it hit me, what do you know?
Give me ten pounds of gold, the kind from
Acapulco!
I stood there for a moment, then... poof it was
there,
A very, sweet fragrance soon filled the air.
I was so happy, I didn't have a care,
Then Jeannie asked me, "Would you like a
damsel so fair?"

I replied, "Why not... make it two dozen?"
"Make them all beautiful...perhaps they're all cousins?"
I'll have for myself, the most beautiful harem,
When my friends drop by, I won't mind sharing 'em.
As I stood there pondering,
What else I should wish for,
There came a loud knocking,
Knocking at my door.
As I was walking across,
My living room floor,
The door burst wide open,
I'll tell you what's more!
It was no other than Willie Nelson,
With a sack of weed in tow,
Willie said, "I come with the weed,
I thought you'd like to know."
"I have the good seed,
They are ready to grow.
We'll plant them in good soil...
In a special way that I know!"
It was then I realized,
What my final wish would be,
Growing' & smokin' with Willie,

Throughout all of eternity!
You might see us out there,
Somewhere just floating around,
We always stay afloat,
Because we never do come down.
Sometimes we write songs,
When there's no one else around,
Look over yonder's Glenn Frey
I guess we're off to "Partytown!"
As soon as we got there,
There being "Partytown",
We were having loads of fun
While only looking around.
We were having ourselves,
One of those high times,
When, who should we stumble into?
None other than Mr. John Prine!
John didn't have a cigarette,
That was nine miles long.
It was actually a joint,
Somehow attached to a water bong.
John joined us as we floated,
Out there amongst the stars,
We all waved to Linda,
As we floated past Mars!

When we reached Pluto,
We told him we saw him as a planet still,
Being told he was a planet again,
Yeah, you could say Pluto was thrilled!
We all float out here together,
We've had a blast right from the start,
When it comes to entertainment,
We each make sure we do our part!

Red Man's Ghost

I wish I'd lived a long time ago,
When the plains were packed with buffalo,
Before the white man came & took command,
Killed off the buffalo... & butchered up the land!

Whoa aho, weep for the Indian,
For when all things are told,
White man came & stole their land,
That's the thing they loved the most!
You can hear it still today,
If you listen real close,
This land is filled with the ancient war-cry,
Of the Red Man's Ghost!

Well, the English came & the French did too,

Red Man stuck in between, wasn't sure what
to do,
Here sign this paper & we'll be friends,
Before the ink dried white man broke the
treaty again.

Whoa aho, I weep for the Indians.
Paradise was stolen away from them,
So, so sad, it truly breaks my heart,
This Eden will never be here again.
You can hear it still today,
If you listen real close,
This land is filled with the ancient war-cry,
Of the Red Man's Ghost!

As the years passed by, Tecumseh knew,
He saw clearly what he needed to do,
He visited every tribe far & wide,
His plan was for them all to unite.
Unite to drive whites back over the
mountains,
There were so many of them it was hard to
count them,
Some tribes joined him in a loose
confederation,

If only he could've united all the Indian
Nations!
Tecumseh might have preserved their
paradise,
For an unknown amount of time,
The world traveled on through space and
time,
Leaving a wonderful way of life behind.
White man's numbers were just too many,
Red Man had very few rifles if they had any.
Yeah, I'm so sad for the indigenous peoples,
White men's ranks grew deeper & deeper,
The whites called them savages, yet it's plain
for me to see,
Red Man was much more civilized... than
whites will ever be,
They took from the land only what was
needed to survive,
White man was, is, & will ever be...the most
savage tribe!

My Young Adult Life

Remembering a time back when I was
seventeen,
There were so many things, my eyes had never
seen,
I was young & wild... free as the breeze,
Wondering about life, if I'd travel overseas.
Wasn't much opportunity... no jobs to be
found,
During the infancy of reaganomics no money
trickled down, (NEVER DID)
One option I had was to join the service,
So I saw my recruiter & enlisted in the Air
Force.
It's the best branch, you know... the best
hands down,

It had long been my dream to escape my hometown.
They flew me down to Lackland AFB, in San Antonio, Texas,
After basic, we rode a bus to Biloxi, in the Airman's Club—we weren't drinking Fresca.
Tech school was great, my classmates & I were tight,
Our instructor we called Yoda, and we, of course, were Jedi Knights!
We all made it through, then we received our orders,
Most of us were sent, beyond our nation's borders.
Yoda had been where we were going, he told us some things he had seen,
We went off to Wallace Air Station in San Fernando, La Union, Philippines.
Before reporting for a year's duty on the other side of the planet,
They offered us thirty days advance leave, we were in no position to demand it.
I was home having fun with family & friends,
Up until my leave was drawing near its end,

One week before my flight on the Flying
Tigers Airline,
KAL007 was shot down, killing many in their
prime.
Shot down by a Russian MIG off the coast of
Japan,
My flight was the next Tuesday on the same
airline with the same flight plan.
We do a lot of things in life we don't really
want to do,
Boarding that 767 in St. Louis was a thing I
had to.
This Airman Basic had his orders, I could not
refuse,
It was then that I believe I paid some heavy
dues.
I'm sure most veterans have had similar
situations,
God bless those who've seen action while
serving our nation!
Well, I made it to the P.I., and obviously
made it back,
My life expectancy was six seconds, if we'd
come under attack,

When I returned stateside, I was at Nellis AFB in Vegas,
The city in the desert, we all called Lost Wages.
I turned nineteen in the Philippine Islands,
I turned twenty in Las Vegas, Nevada,
I was too young to drink off base,
What I heard was Yada, Yada, Yada!
Growing up in West Virginia, the drinking age was eighteen,
To a GI two years older, the fact that I couldn't drink was obscene!
Those who knew me then, knew that I loved beer,
They say I'm ahead of my quota, although I haven't had one in fourteen years!
I hadn't had a beer in eleven months,
When my great friend Greg Garrett passed away,
The last two I drank were with Greg,
I figured I'd leave it that way.

Truer Love

I have loved some women,
A few have loved me back,
They were all so beautiful,
I came from the wrong side of the tracks.
They were all so amazing,
Each in her own special way,
Their remembrance brings fond memories,
Of better times & happier days.
If I could go back in time,
Relive those days again,
Would I do anything differently,
Or once again piss into the wind?
Perhaps I should've settled down,
Gotten married & put down roots,
I've always been a tumbleweed,

Grass doesn't grow around my boots!
Some people plan a trip down to the finest details,
I fly by the seat of my pants, letting the wind fill my sails.
I love feeling the freedom of traveling down a road,
No one anywhere is freer than a free-spirited nomadic hobo!
I know it's not for everyone to always be on the go,
I've never liked just sitting around or doing what I'm told!
I never liked being tied down, except for that one time,
I wonder where she is today, she'd completely slipped my mind.
She was a special Lady, she kept her ropes just right,
She never let them get loose & they never were too tight.
She led me around on her leash, yet her leash was long,
Giving the illusion of freedom, while her hold on me was strong.

How I got away from her, I truly cannot say,
I don't know how it happened... How did I get away?
Maybe this is why I travel, why I always move along,
To keep her from catching me, I wish I knew what she had in that bong!
If she catches up to me, will I be turned into a boll weevil?
She may have been a witch, although her heart was not evil.
She was just so darn sweet, a real-life practical joker,
She loved to laugh & laughed at love, a well-balanced emotions broker.
My hobo days are over, never realized how I missed her,
Wonder if she's on my trail, if she liked the way I kissed her?
Guess I'll slow my pace down; if she's coming, she will find me,
God knows I love that woman, even her ropes that bind me!

Yes, she loved to laugh, and she laughed at love,
Her heart fit mine like a custom-made glove.
We were great together, never spoke one cross word,
We thought it'd last forever which was naive & absurd!
People often grow,
People sometimes change,
Then we face the times,
When our lives get rearranged.
Love should always come easy,
True love is never strained,
Step easy & tread lightly,
Love is all that remains!
She was really a living Doll,
Super sweet & so charming,
That she'd had her eye on me,
I somehow found this quite alarming.
She was so full of life,
Spontaneous & carefree,
How could this gorgeous angel,
Looked twice at a devil like me?

West Virginia Sunshine

The sunshine's brighter in West Virginia,
I know this to be true,
The sun shines brighter in West Virginia,
Want me to prove it to you?
I can do this on two conditions,
First, you must be sane in your thinking,
Second & more important, (since we are all
crazy)
You must use logic when you're reasoning.

West Virginia is almost heaven,
You can't deny this, it's in a song,
Which makes us closer to the sun,
The sun shines brighter, I'm not wrong.
Sol's sunbeams, rays, & energy,
All reach West Virginia first!
You all get what's leftover,
After our crops quench their thirst.

It is logical since God visits often,
Fresh mountain air & clear running streams,
Why would He go to a sand-mired, salty
beach,
When He created for us, the place of His
dreams!
The people are really nice here,
The friendliest you'll meet by far,
Even on dreary days when it rains,
We get sunshine from root-cellar jars!
That's why we're nice & friendly,
The way God intended mankind to be,
Us Mountaineers Are Always Free,
As first proclaimed in 1863!
Our crops grow abundantly beneath these
Blue-Ridge skies,
Our past-time is watching white puffy clouds
float by,
Sometimes we float on them—if we're really
high,
The logic makes perfect sense—come on over
& give it a try!
Florida (The Sunshine State) ain't got nothing
on us,

Rising water levels & hurricanes can sure be a bust,
If you want to relax come & visit us,
West Virginia's really laid-back so you might have to adjust.

Death

Death comes for us all,
We cannot escape.
You know this is true,
One might choke eating a grape..
Sure there've been some,
Whose own death they've faked.
Death calls on them too,
Possibly in an earthquake.

Death calls on us all in time,
These earthly bodies we leave behind.
Our soul & spirit fly beyond the stars,
In death we gain immortality by far.
Death brings illumination, not dark,
Do not fear the journey on which we will all embark.
Our family & friends, we leave with broken hearts.

If only they could see us, making our brand new start.

Death brings no darkness,
In death we become light.
Oh how eager I am,
To lift off in flight.
To enter outer space,
In the light of a million stars.
Not sure if we'll have wings,
We won't need flying cars.
Floating past the red planet,
Commonly known as Mars.
We used to hold these discussions,
Back when I hung out in bars.

No Guarantee

If you have a beautiful body,
There's no guarantee you'll win the prize;
Sure, it may help you in this world,
Your soul is where true beauty lies.
The gateway to the soul,
Lies directly behind your eyes;
It isn't easy to discern,
Harder still to scrutinize.
If the aura which surrounds you,
Glows golden with a silver hue;
I'd say your soul is beautiful,
Which makes you a beautiful person too!
We're not a body that has a soul,
We're a soul that has a body;
This body one day will return to dust,
This is fact, not an anomaly.
Our souls and spirits travel on,

They're not to this earth bound;
Travel out beyond the stars,
Our bodies return to the ground.
Some say this life is all we have,
I cannot swallow that;
Is the moon actually made from cheese?
Is the earth actually flat?
Don't jump at me, flat-earthers,
Your beliefs mean nothing to me;
Do you also believe the sun and moon are flat,
Not round as all eyes can see?
The beauty in a sunrise,
Brings a new day's dawning;
Each day gives a chance to start anew,
Don't allow your past to come haunting.
It's okay at times to look ahead,
If you're not overtly flaunting;
Plans are made that may fall through,
Boasts are often daunting.
If you have to boast and brag,
Tell people how great you are;
You my friend have missed the boat,
Being humble is better by far.
Maybe you love compliments,
They're as easily given as received;

Someone once said that talk is cheap,
Is this a truth to be believed?
If you care what others think of you,
You can be easily deceived;
They'll tell you what you want to hear,
You might wish you'd never been conceived.
I'm not saying all compliments are bad,
Some are sincere and from the heart;
Be wary of those who give compliments,
Their will they may try to impart.
Not everyone you meet,
Will have ulterior motives;
There might be more than we'd expect,
End results could be explosive.
I don't like negative thoughts,
So I'll leave you on an upbeat;
You never know what someone's going through,
Be gentle and kind to those you greet!
There are better days that lie ahead,
Good will always prevail;
Keep this in mind and persevere,
Live on to tell the tale!

Mistletoe

Do you know what this is, she asked
I replied that it looked like oral sex mistletoe,
But I thought I was the only one,
Who knows the only place it grows.
Said she'd followed me one day,
Just to see where I'd go.
Said it surprised her when I walked straight,
When I came to the fork in the road.
Oh my goodness!
That took balls,
Would you like for me to show you,
The best mistletoe of all?
What could be better,
Than oral sex on demand?
It's really so much better,

Than doing it by hand.
The best mistletoe of all,
Will take you to the one who loves you most.
You might not even know them,
It somehow searches coast to coast.
This is how I came to be here,
All alone with you now.
She said since I came to her,
She'd been wondering exactly how?
I got into her bedroom, inside of her locked house.
She was going to ask about this,
She was glad I was there anyhow.
This is sort of like that mistletoe,
That one you were telling me about.
Except it brings to you the one,
Who loves you most in this nation.
So you see, you came to be here,
By two separate incantations.
Incantations we both learned,
Using rote memorization.
As soon as I learned mine,
I cast it without any hesitation.
Oh, I see now it was you,
You brought me by your invitation.

I knew my warlock powers,
Were never really that strong.
I'd been thinking you might like me,
I was hoping I wasn't wrong.
Tell me, did your spell mention,
Smoking from a water bong?
Does it also have to be a bong,
Bought online from one Tommy Chong?
How did you know that detail?
Have you been tailing me all along?
No Baby, I swear I haven't,
Please believe me, it's the truth
Allow me to explain, Dear,
I have a confession too.
Please hear me out, my love,
I will prove it to you.
The book of spells you found,
I had left it for you to peruse.
The man you met in the park that day,
Well you see, that was also yours truly
I'd become so smitten by you,
I needed to know your love fully..
I'm the man who sold to you
The awesome water bong,
Told you it'd once belonged,

To the infamous pothead, Tommy Chong.
One more confession I have for you,
Dave has been here all along.
In fact it was his bong I sold you,
I don't know if he knows it's gone.
What? What's that? You already knew?
How can this be when I just made up,
Everything I just told you?
I'm a witch, remember?
More powerful than you'll ever be.
I can read your thoughts as if,
They're displayed on a big-screen TV.

That's when I woke up,
It had all been a dream.
In my dream I was asleep,
Dreaming of this scene.
I was all alone in my house,
Suddenly she was there.
I shit you not!
She came right out of thin air!
How did you get here?
How'd you come out of that plant?
Why does it matter?
It's really insignificant.

Forgive me, Dearest,
For I have just awakened.
When you appeared like that,
You shook my mental foundation.
She answered me,
Being so nonchalant.
You forgot I'm a witch,
I pop in when and where I want.
Samantha my love,
I thought I'd been dreaming.
Can you tell me, Dear,
Does this all have any meaning?
That's when I woke up again,
I was going deaf from the screaming!
Now it's out there on YouTube,
As it is continuously streaming.
What is it that you say?
You didn't find this entertaining?
I'm sorry, I get all these thoughts,
At times only the wrong ones are remaining.
I honestly don't know,
How this story ends.
If my thoughts cycle back,
I'll gladly fill you in.

One more thing, I have a disclaimer,
I used the name Samantha you see,
'Cause I've always crushed on my favorite witch,
Miss Elizabeth Montgomery.

Missing Dallas

It's been six years,
Since I heard your laugh;
I miss hearing it,
There are no doubts about that!
At times I find myself,
Remembering a time when;
You'd say 'Vah-nii-laaahhh,'
With a big ole grin.
I can't go back there,
Back to that time;
So I travel through time & space,
Time travelling in my mind.
You were a prince of a boy, Dallas,
Some people thought you were mine;
You were the same to me,

And that was all just fine!
I can hear your laugh,
When Bob played you the Ice Cream Song;
You'd giggle & giggle at the end
At the cone taking a slurp of the dog.
You really liked Bob,
I wish he was still around town;
But then he wouldn't have been there to meet you,
To look after you & show you around.
Another old friend was once your neighbor,
I'm certain you remember Greg;
We'd put you through his bathroom window,
Probably landing on your head.
I remember when you opened the door,
You looked up at Greg like the other times before;
This time you asked him if he had a spare key,
To give it to your mom so she could unlock your door.
Garrett looked at me, saying from the mouths of babes,
Then he asked why we didn't think of that?
I replied Big D's pretty sharp,
Greg said you had a head like a house cat!

You couldn't have been more than 5 or 6,
I thought there was no way you'd ever top
this;
Little did I know, Dallas had something up
his sleeve,
I still laugh out loud ‘til I almost piss.
One Sunday morning Greg called for a ride to
town,
It most certainly was a "Sunday Morning
Coming Down;"
I walked over to Garrett's while Mom was
getting you,
That's when you said it...right out of the blue.
When you saw Greg you asked why he was
going to town,
This part is classic, I laugh so hard still;
You looked up at Garrett & told him,
"If you're looking for your truck it's in the
ditch at the bottom of the hill."
Spoken with a Boone County accent,
From where you were always around Mom;
You said it matter-of-factly,
With such grace & aplomb.
Greg & I laughed about that,
Up til the day that he died;

You gained his respect,
When you hadn't even tried!
You were a natural,
So naturally cool;
You stood up for weaker kids,
Never once did I see you be cruel.
A huge gaping void,
Was created when you left;
It'll never be filled,
We're all still sad & bereft.
No it will never be filled,
Until we're all with you again;
You were good at so many things,
You were best at being a friend!
I miss you so much,
This world will never be the same;
We go on as best we can,
I still look up when I hear your name.
God, it hurts so bad,
It literally breaks my heart;
I wonder if we knew the price of love,
Would any of us ever start?
Yeah, six years have passed,
It never gets any easier;
If there's any change at all,

My poems might get a little cheesier.
I miss you Big D,
You're always in my thoughts;
What's more & more important,
You are forever in my heart!

Love you, Dallas.

Sixty

Sixty is coming,
It's right around the corner,
Winter's coming too,
Might go someplace warmer.
I'm about due for a road trip,
A long, strange excursion,
A Long, Strange Trip,
The 2024 version.
Might mosey out towards Frisco,
See if Haight-Ashbury is still around,
It'd be cool to check out,
The old stomping grounds!
I reckon sixty is a milestone,
It hasn't seemed that long!
I feel the same age as always,
Only my aches & pains prove me wrong.

Once I get to moving,
It's sometimes hard to slow me down,
I don't know how this will sound,
Maybe it's time for me to slow down.

Where did that come from?
You're not old, you've only begun,
See, that right there is proof,
I really am as crazy as I look!
Sitting here conversing with myself,
I sure don't see anyone else,
Well, we know we're not hallucinating,
That'd be a different scene we'd be creating.
Why have we never had this conversation
before?
I guess you never knocked on my door.
I didn't knock on your door today either!
Why not? I've always wanted to meet a
cheater.
Hey now! Where'd you go?
I just met you & now you've gone ghost.
Well, there's a fine 'Howdy Do?'
I'll talk to myself... like I used to.
Imagine if you will,
Having someone to talk to & not knowing,

I talk back to the cattle when they're lowing.
They give good advice always,
They're good listeners every day.
If that guy comes back again,
I'm going to ask him where he went,
If he ever goes back again,
I want to go along with him.

Ole Dude came to say goodbye,
I had to ask him the reason why?
He told me it was his fault, not mine,
I asked him just what was his crime?
He had spoken to me aloud,
This was strictly not allowed,
He was that wee voice when I was whole,
The voice of my conscience & my soul.
Where was he going? I had to know,
One can't just lose their conscience & their soul,
He said he really didn't know,
That he hadn't actually been told.
Love your life & everything in it,
Live your life & be a blessing to those in it.
It's not a competition... you can't win it,
God will bless you back if you begin it.

Unless, of course, that's the reason you do it,
God knows everything so you can't lie to
Him,
God is everywhere so you can't fool Him.
Just do unto others,
As you'd have them do to you,
Then he said something,
About a foot in another shoe.
When God came, I ran & asked Him,
If I could have my soul & conscience back
again?
God said he'd allow it if I didn't make any
waves,
I said, "Lord, you know I always behave."
That's when I heard a most thunderous laugh,
God told me I could've said anything but that.
I promised God I'd really behave,
My soul & conscience needed to be saved
That's when I heard the wee voice again,
We'd made acquaintances and now we were
friends.
It seems I've known him a really long time,
It's like maybe, for my whole life!
I tried, but I couldn't let it go,
Now I've told you that a man can have no

conscience or soul,
I guess I'll do as I am told,
Sometimes it sucks growing old.
Some of ya'll might think I've lost my mind,
I just search my brain for words that rhyme,
At times they are hard to find,
Other times they make nonsensical rhymes.
I still can't let it go,
'Cause I'm true blue,
donald j trump,
Will make a fool of you!
Plus you'll probably end up doing time,
donald j trump is a no-good, low-down louse!

Sometimes they don't have to rhyme.

Hope you all have a happy, joyous lap,
Your next trip around the sun!

Mom, Happy belated Birthday! I Love You

Mom, you were the first woman I ever loved in this world,
Sister Joy was the next and then little sister Trish,
Along the way, Mom, I've loved a few girls,
A few of them turned out to be a real bitch.
Then there was MawMaw Hazel and MawMaw Pauline,
When we reunite in Heaven, won't it be a glorious scene?

I know I caused troubles and heartaches over the years,
I hope some of the good things, make up for your tears.

I sure was a little bit wild way back in the day,
A little? How 'bout
a lot; it just seemed to be my way.

You were always there for me,
In the good times and the bad;
You were my Mom, my Rock,
Let me tell you, I sure was glad!
I sure found it easy,
To get out and get in trouble;
You and Dad bailed me out,
More times than just a couple.
Don't know what I'd have done without you,
Or where I'd be now;
When I look back on it all,
All I can say is WOW!

I know you and some others,
Must've prayed for me a lot;
To quit raisin' hell and drinkin' beer,
To act and behave how I'd been taught.
I sure did some things,
Sometimes I got caught;
You were always the same,
No matter my lot.

You're the best cook,
The best cook hands down,
Greg Garrett's wife asked him,
Why the McDonald's biscuits were so good in our town.
I think you know what Greg told her—
He told her that's because Geno's mom makes 'em!
Your peanut butter fudge?
That's a whole 'nother anthem.
Your hamburgers taste better,
Than any I've ever had;
Your potato salad too,
Your food's never been bad.
Unless you forget to add sugar,
When you're making pumpkin pies;
I threw that in for Dad,
I know it made him smile. ;-)

I guess what I'm tryin' to say,
Is thanks for all your love;
Your love's unconditional,
Like God's in Heaven above.
Thank you for your guidance,

For correcting me when I did wrong;
If I'd learned to play guitar,
I'd have written you a song.

I'm sorry this is late,
Your birthday was two days ago;
That's the thing about writing,
When it comes.
I love you so much, Mom,
Love you with all my heart;
You're the best woman I ever met,
I knew that right from the start!
–

In memory of Dallas Logan Clark December 29,1995-September 7,2018

Five Years

If you're looking five years ahead,
It may seem a very long time;
Time goes by awfully fast.
When you're looking at five years behind,
Time is only a relative thing,
Made up in the minds of mankind;
Time can also be irrelevant,

Slipping by in the twinkling of an eye.

Five years have now passed,
Since you departed this life;
It doesn't seem possible,
Five years can't be right.
I miss your smile,
Your charm and your wit;
I miss your laugh,
And that look I'd sometimes get.

Oft times I find myself,
Daydreaming and wishing;
You were still here,
We're gettin' ready to go fishing.
We always caught fish,
We caught other things too;
Most times I wish,
I could just hang out with you.

It's all so surreal,
This thing we call time;
It still breaks my heart,
You were taken in your prime.
You had a kind heart,

A heart good as gold;
You'll never have to feel,
The aches and pains of growing old.
They say the good die young,
Dallas you were one of the best;
My nephew, my friend, I miss you,
The time we had with you, we were blessed.

This old world keeps on turning,
We all keep plodding along;
Through good times and bad,
Seeing the right and the wrong.
You're never far from my thoughts,
You're always top on my chart;
I can often sense your presence,
You are forever in my heart. .
You've seen things we can't imagine,
Yes we all miss you down here;
It just doesn't seem possible,
Has it been five years? Happy Birthday
Dallas!!!!!
You are Twenty-Eight this year;
I really enjoyed our little chat,
Good to see PawPaw with you there.
It was so great to see,

That BIG smile on your face;
We all miss you down here,
It sure ain't the same place.
PawPaw Virgil, and MawMaw Pauline;
Standing beside you and Dad,
It truly was, a most beautiful scene!
We will all be together,
Again one of these days;
Joy gave me one of your keyboards,
I'm gonna learn how to play.
You really looked great!
Especially the SHINE!
I'll let everyone know,
You ARE doing just fine.
Joy & Haley miss you like crazy,
We all do as a matter of fact;
I'll be with you 'fore long,
Hopefully, I'll arrive...fully intact.

Love Ya BIG D!!!! It's been six years.

Leave it all Behind

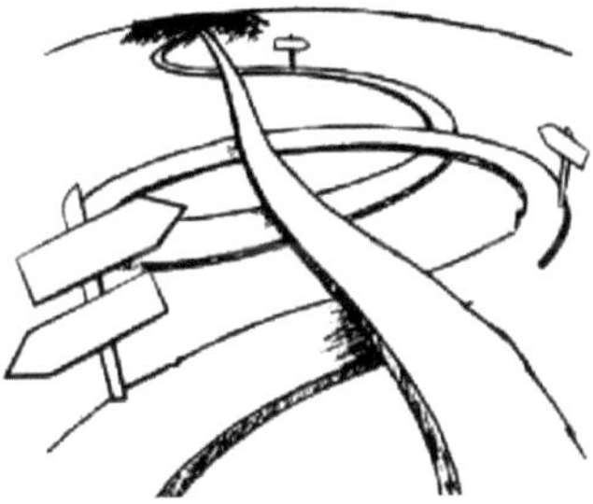

Let's leave everything behind,
Leave it behind like time out of mind.
After all, those aren't your hills to climb,
They may have been...once upon a time.

You've gone off and taken some other way,
Your sense of direction is now on display.
People no longer care what we might have to say,
Our time will come, it's just not today.

There are times in our lives when we face delays,
Always remember to give the Good Lord His praise.
What we are going through is just another phase,

What lies ahead can only be better days!

We'll all stick together, now & always,
Good things will come, to all those who pray.
Never cared much about what anyone says,
Why do you suppose Shriners wear a fez?

Never allow yourself to grow smug &
complacent,
Do you have any idea what is growing in your
basement?
Would you ever give the police an official
statement?
Only to open yourself up to abuse &
debasement.

What bizarro world to ours lies adjacent?
Some only look on in grandiose amazement.
Do you even know your earthly placement?
Is graffiti on walls a form of defacement?

We'll always move forward as we know we
must,
Who the Hell gives a fuck about Elon Musk?
The hour is growing late...it soon will be dusk,

Did you ever hear the one about ole such &
such?

It seems like his lies are never-ending,
Most are far beyond my rational
comprehending.
Do any of your fences ever need mending?
What message to the children do you think
we are sending?

Sometimes it's okay to tell lies, situation
depending,
It's okay, the rules sometimes need bending.
Befriending tyrants & autocrats, I find
apprehensive,
Being known by the company you keep, many
now find offensive.
Don't worry it's not your money you've been
spending,
Keep borrowing more for as long as they keep
lending.
Many transactions are perpetually pending,
Does your checkbook ever need careful
scrutiny and tending?

Have you walked the path that now is
wending?
Are the hypocrites the ones you enjoy
offending?
Is it to new heights you are ascending?
Do truth & lies now seem to be blending?

Why are arrogant people so condescending?
Are the gathering fascists all now attending?
Will they ever be apprehended?
Is it the grapes of wrath that now are
fermenting?

Nobody wants to help out one another,
Who gives a shit, he ain't my brother.
Would you say the same about your very own
mother?
It is above your deathbed that your spirit
hovers.

One day very soon you'll be under the clover,
Don't even ask, we don't grant do-overs.
Do you remember playing Red Rover, Red
Rover?
Have you ever been told to simply bend over?

Pull up a seat and we'll have us a palaver,
Are you now or have you ever spoken with a cadaver?

,
If so,was the cadaver as mad as a hatter?
Did you only discuss subjects that really matter?

Have you ever had your hopes & dreams completely shattered?
Do you like to eat shrimp that's deep-fried & battered?
Have you ever heard tiny footsteps go pitter-patter?
Ever faced your demons & then watched them scatter?

We must hold true & maintain our course,
Keep moving forward, never showing remorse.
We must keep looking, continue our search,
If we're to save our planet, God's own green earth.

Take all my words for what they are worth,
My words could scarcely be called a dearth.
They keep on coming from wherever they're birthed,
If I ever get writer's block it will surely come with mirth.

This poem is filled with nonsensical rhymes,
I just never know which hills I will climb.
One thing I know is I've had a good time,
If you've read to the end, you must find my words sublime.

Death of the Constitution

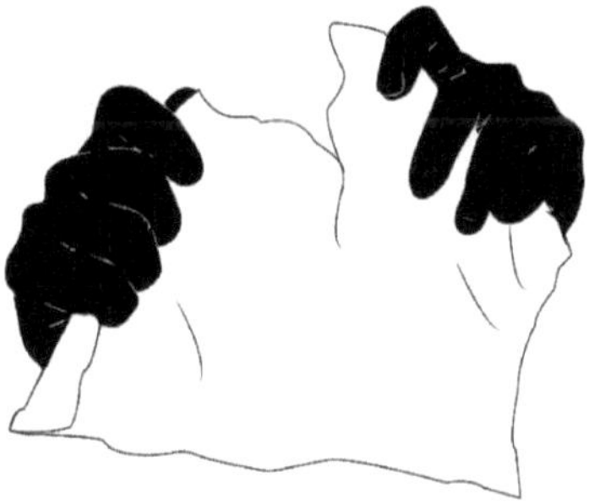

I wonder who will be inspired,
When once again, Orange Stain is fired.
All those with whom he conspired,
Should everyone be permanently retired?
Instead of holding cabinet positions,
All their asses should be in prison.
Should his plan come to fruition,
We will know our duty, and our mission.
No longer will we make our own decisions,
We will become their dereliction.
Tyrannical Dictatorship is their objective,
Their facts are in fact merely subjective.
To abolish the Constitution,
Will bring all opposition to destitution.
The right to protest will disappear,

They seek to rule by mongering fear.
Make no mistake, let this be clear,
The Resistance has been and will always be here!
We will survive these next four years,
It's for future generations whom we endear.
We must stand strong, showing no fear,
Keep the faith & remain in good cheer.
For ourselves, we are not concerned,
The trump flags should all be burned.
So ludicrous...so unpatriotic,
These next four years will be despotic & chaotic.
Despotic & Chaotic!
The MAGA drones are hypnotic & psychotic.
Hypnotic & Psychotic!
Unable to form a cognitive thought,
They cannot see the evil that they have wrought.
They seek not that which should be sought,
They stand for what our military has always fought.
The Orange Stain brought this dilemma,
He should be given a truth serum enema!
Perhaps then he could speak the truth,

Until then, this whole point is moot.
We'll stand toe to toe, each and every day,
Linked arm in arm we will not betray.
We'll defend the Constitution—hip hip
Hooray!
Simply because, we love the U.S. of A.!!!!

The Grand Experiment

Has the grand experiment truly failed?
Are we incapable of governing ourselves?
The wealthy, it seems always get their own way,
It's the poor schmucks like us,
Who pay while they play!
They seldom if ever give anything in return,
We barely scrape by, they've got money to burn.
Justice is blind...so I've been told,
We're supposed to be equal...all cast from one mold.
Doesn't look that way to me...as I grow old(er).
The rich and the powerful call themselves elite,

All of us peons are to bow down at their feet.
They think they can do anything, that they
can break any law,
They mock us and taunt us like we're the ones
flawed.
The time has come to resist, time to put them
in their place;
My friends, if we don't, we'll crash and burn
in disgrace.
What's right for me is right for you too,
Some blur the lines of what's false and what's
true.
He's "The Father of Lies," give the Devil his
due,
Beware at all times 'cause he will deceive you.
Glory and power are his desire...who would
you think of? Someone who seeks fame,
"I'm the only one...ME ME ME" the only one,
you can believe.
"Don't believe what you see, or what you hear
with your own ears,
I only speak the truth, it will all be made
clear."
"I deal in absolutes, you can be absolutely
certain,

I'm just a puppet, my masters behind the curtain.
"I'm the Chosen One, Chosen by Satan,
To cede to Putin this once proud nation.
No other man, in all of God's creation,
Could make you see truth as your imagination."
If he ever spoke the truth, it might sound something like that,
He'd admit he's a vile, despicable treasonous asshat.
Not only him, but so many others,
Sold us all down the river for cheap Russian rubles..
I tell you not a single one of them,
Has one bit of scruples.
They gave tours to their minions, and had them do their bidding;
Making them believe all the while what they were doing was winning!
It's time to arrest, all of these treasonous traitors;
I'd like to send them all off...to meet their Creator.
If we don't hold righteous judgement, as

instructed by God;
If we don't send 'em all to prison,
Our system's grievously flawed!
There will be no more order, no rule of law;
It's so easy to see, MAGAS why can't ya'll?
A set of strict rules for us, while they literally
get away with murder;
We can't allow this to go, not one bit further!
Lord smite them down, allow good to prevail.
Evil is running rampant all over the earth.
While many sit by watching, not caring,
What do they think their freedom is worth?
How they ignore injustice I will never
understand,
I just can't do that, I'm not that kind of man.
The kind of man who can watch children's
hospitals being bombed,
Then say Vladimir Putin's my friend, he's not
doing wrong!
It truly disturbs me that in the land of the
free,
So many among us can agree to disagree.
How do you do that? I'd really love to know;
When basic human rights are taken away
blow after blow.

There are certain truths on which we all should agree
Such as the pursuit of happiness, life, and liberty!
When these are challenged, I can't agree to disagree.
Russia invaded Ukraine, Putin wants parts of their land,
He has no rights to it, but he gave the command.
trump called him a genius, for invading a sovereign land;
For putting into motion his evil schemes and loathsome plans.
In Putin, trump sees what he himself longs to be,
A despot, a dictator driven by his greed.
Back when I was a kid we didn't tolerate this shit,
When proven guilty, they chose to acquit!
Take the truth and twist it to fit your concern,
Who taught them this, where did they learn?
The answer is found in the place we call Hell,
Satan himself is behind that thin veil.

Good is now evil...evil is good,
So many are blinded, if I could make them see, I would.
Our country and the world, are so interwoven,
We are the world's police whether we choose to be or not,
Whether we want to or not, it really doesn't matter.
We must stand up to Putin's evil plot!
The world looks to us to lead, and lead with integrity;
How can we do this, and allow traitors to walk around free?
They act like it doesn't matter, all the damage they've caused,
Treason must be punished, traitors should be shot!!
I know they've changed the law, firing squads are not allowed;
We must follow the law, because we ain't like that crowd.
What I'd love to kill, what would leave me so enheartened;
Would be to see trump's ego crushed, his

spirit stoned, broken unpardoned.
Co-conspirators too, they need to pay the Piper,
They're no better than trump, wearing a diaper!
Going down the toilet, and straight onto hell;
That's where our country's headed,
I guess time will tell.
One thing I know for certain, although it may never happen;
The MAGAS need to get WOKE before they sell off Manhattan!
Yet they believe the propaganda and the lies;
I've no idea how to reach them, although I've often wanted to try.
It's really so disheartening, it's really very sad;
They don't want to know the truth, know it'll make them look bad.
Good news MAGAS, you can't possibly look worse,
Than how you look now, doting on the rear end of a horse!

Wake up and get WOKE, soon you'll be

feeling better,
About yourself and life, and everything that matters.
I hope you will reunite with us
to prosecute these traitors,
Do it for your children's children, those who'll follow later.
Majority rules, and I sincerely hope it remains,
To give all decisions to anyone is foolish; to trump? it's insane!!!
He only cares about himself, of this you can be sure,
What's in it for him, for his greed there is no cure.
He can never have enough, there's many more with this disease;
What do they think they'll take, when this world they leave?
What a pathetic life, to keep more than what you gave.
Always wanting more, it's "everything" they crave,
No matter how they get it, or the way they must behave.

Truly little children, in emotion, thought, and ways,
It's passed the point of being called a phase.
Actually little babies, wanting every whim fulfilled,
They don't give a shit who has to be killed.
I wonder when they'll grow up, ripen, and mature;
Start acting like grown adults, instead of horse manure.
I know I strayed from the subject, and rambled on and on...
We must punish treason, if we don't, all hope is gone.

Not a Christian Nation

When all things are taken,
Into consideration.
The United States has never once been,
What you'd call a Christian nation.
Your people might have landed,
At Plymouth Rock.
If you're all hoity-toity,
This might come as a shock.
When babies are born,
It is for knowledge they thirst.
By the gaining of this knowledge,
There are some who will be hurt.
Of all the people,
Here on planet Earth.
There's not one group of people,
For whom Jesus died first.
It's said that He gave His life,

Willingly to save all of mankind.
For every person who ever lived,
Since the very beginning of time.
So please don't ever think you are better,
Than another human being.
Although there are some of us who are blessed,
For believing without seeing.
I have never seen Noah's Ark,
But I believe that's when rain began,
The first time rain fell upon the land.
Whether you believe or not,
Actually does mean a lot!
While we are still here,
My duty is to see that you're taught.
I cannot teach you,
From my grave.
Jesus Christ gave His life,
For your soul to save.
The Bible says,
There is no other way.
To come to the Father,
Call on Jesus' name & you shall be saved.
You can have the gift,
Of eternal life.

By asking Jesus to forgive you,
All will be set right.
The gift is free,
You cannot pay with gold. .
Jesus gave His life,
To save our very souls.

Our Nation's Last Gleaming

Oh, say can you see,
Our nation's last gleaming?
This would be a nightmare,
If only I were dreaming.
Orange Stain's proposed cabinet,
Is positively daunting.
Unqualified & corrupt,
I sense Hitler's ghost haunting.

The very oxymorons,
Of the departments they'll be heading.
MAGA, can you see now,
A second term we are dreading?
Orange Shitstain has made a mockery,
Of our institutions.
The fox guarding the henhouse—

Draw your own conclusions.
I assure you that none of this,
Is hyperbole or illusion.
Orange one should be disqualified,
That'd be the best solution.
What bothers me most,
What really draws my ire.
It that MAGA thinks we made it up,
That we only sit around & conspire.
I'll tell them something about chump,
They'll say they didn't know that.
To which I reply I know,
Or else you'd drop him flat!
I really don't get it,
I guess they're just too lazy.
The plain truth is out there,
Very clear & not at all hazy.
They shuffle along blindly,
Struggling through life.
Claiming they're all the same,
That all politicians lie.
I guess we all lie,
About one thing or the other.
Yet flat-out telling lie,
After lie, after lie—oh brother!

Over 30,000 lies,
His first term in office.
Averaging around twenty a day,
Many of which were pointless.

Some claim to be Christians,
Yeah, they say they're believers.
How can this be?
When you openly support a deceiver?
If you've read the Bible,
If you know what it said.
How can you stand behind,
One who turns it all on its head?
He has claimed to be,
The second coming of Jesus, (the two
coming?)
Isn't it much easier to believe,
Satan sent him to deceive us?
Yeah, The Father of Lies,
Reigns over this earth.
It's in the scriptures,
For what that is worth.
Ya'll pick and choose,
Which scriptures you believe.
I guess "love thy neighbor,"

Is like water through a sieve.
Colossians 3:31—do not neglect,
Hospitality to strangers.
Some have entertained angels unawares,
To not do so brings danger
Romans 13:8 Love does no wrong to a
neighbor,
Therefore love fulfills the law.
Separating families at our border,
You think that is love, PSHAW!
Who are the ones who are hurt,
When they blindly give their support?
They harm us all,
For all that is worth it.
Back when I was going to church,
They spoke of God removing His blessing.
From the U.S. of A. blaming all,
While the real reason went by without
addressing.
Thomas Jefferson said he shuddered,
When he thought about God being just.
The treatment of Indigenous peoples,
Should shame us all into dust.
I'm not claiming to be better,
Than any MAGA supporters.

I'm merely more informed,
By truth-telling reporters.
We have Reagan to thank,
For news stations spreading lies.
For some reason he wanted this—
Ask an Irani or Contra why.
Reagan committed election interference,
By asking Iran not to release the hostages,
Until after he was elected president,
The Constitution still feels the damages!
The war machine was unhappy,
They weren't making any money.
President Jimmy Carter,
Never dropped one bomb on anybody!
To them this was unacceptable,
This peacenik could not remain in office.
The GOP claims to be the "Christian Party,"
Yet the ones they put in only accost us!
The GOP is rotten, rotten to its core,
They only care about war, and taking money from the poor.
Their unquenched greed is never satisfied,
All they want is more, more, more!
They don't care how they get it,
They'll be anybody's whore.

Only one thing makes them happier,
When money comes with a side order of
blood, guts, and gore!

The Rise of King Richard

There once lived a king,
In a faraway land.
His hobbies included,
The selling of contraband.
Travelers would come,
From near & far.
To trade with the king,
Whom some say came from Mars.
He may have been a time traveler,
Headed towards his destination.
He simply wouldn't tolerate,
Any woman's exploitation.
For this very reason,
The women loved him.

That's not why he stood up for them,
In his heart of hearts, he adored them.
He always thought things through,
The king never acted rashly on a whim.
One secret the king kept—
He'd never learned how to swim.
No one ever knew his secret,
What's that? How do I know?
You're getting ahead of my story,
You little so & so.
Okay, where was I?
Oh yeah, the king couldn't swim.
No one ever knew his secret,
'Cause I...er the king never told a living soul.
The dead & undead,
It is okay to tell.
If they begin to tell someone,
You can send them back to Hell.
That's how I got it figured,
Near as I can tell.
An angel does gain its wings,
Each time you hear a bell.

There was never any trouble,
In this faraway land.

Where once lived a king,
Who dealt in contraband.
He loved to get high,
He enjoyed smoking marijuana.
He shared with his people,
They could get high if they wanted.
Which is another reason,
His people all loved him.
The king never had,
A greedy bone in his body.
If one of his people got sick,
He doctored them with hot toddies!
As the king saw himself,
He was just a nobody.
He never thought too highly of himself,
But man, the king loved to party!
Yeah, the king loved to party,
Yet remained within his limitations.
The king's limitations you see,
Made no mention of moderation.
Then one day a flood came,
The people were all running around.
When the flood finally receded,
The people realized the king had drowned.
The price of keeping a secret,

May include your own life.
So whatever you do,
Never tell a secret to your wife.
That's how Prince Richard,
Came to be in power.
He became King Richard,
During the land's darkest hour.
If King Richard found out,
You were an exploiter of women.
You didn't get a second chance,
With the fishes, you'd be swimmin'.

Real Love

Jesus remained on that cross,
As He was suffering & bleeding.
Only because He knew,
How much we all would need Him.
The full weight of this world,
Was placed squarely upon His shoulders.
He could have easily slain,
Each & every Roman soldier.
Jesus did what He knew,
To be the will of His Father.
Selflessly Jesus gave His life,
As He knew there would be no other.
Doing the Father's will is truly,
Why His judgement is just.
We will all stand in judgement before Jesus,
Silently guilty, yes we will, each one of us.

As Jesus looked over the crowd there
gathered,
He saw James standing beside Mary, His
mother.
The tortured, anguished pain they saw in His
eyes,
Was too much for Mary, & James, His
step-brother.
They couldn't force their tears, to remain in
their eyes,
This I understand, so many times I have cried.
His unconditional love for us,
Is what held Him on that cross,
For our ransom had to be paid,
Jesus paid a tremendous cost!!!
Jesus entered this world,
To seek & to save that which was lost..
Jesus descended from Heaven to save our
souls,
It was He whom Satan had tried to accost.
If Jesus would only bow down,
To Lucifer, kneeling at his feet,
He'd be given this entire world,
Not once experiencing the taste of defeat.

Jesus was the only begotten Son,
Of God our Father.
He knew this fell to Him,
There would never be another,
For this reason, He left His place,
At the right hand of the Father.
He hadn't come down to Earth,
Only to make wine out of water.
Doing not His will, but the will of His Father,
Again...makes His judgement just.
God the Father, God the Son, God the Holy Ghost,
Form the Trinity of the God...I truly trust.

To our human, finite minds,
This is beyond all comprehension.
We cannot understand,
Infinite, omniscient wisdom.
There are those who claim,
Three cannot make one.
While they fail to see,
This already has been done.
A human being must think,
Extremely highly of themselves.
To think they know more than God,

These people need a padded cell.

No earthly inhabitant has a clue,
As to what all is going on.
A thing we all may learn,
In its entirety before too long.
Only the Father knows,
How long He will allow us to go on.
How much longer will it last,
Before this world is gone?
Not the angels in Heaven above,
Nor the demons in Hell below,
Not the Holy Ghost, nor Jesus,
Only God the Father knows.
We can see that time,
The Earth's time is running short.
To judge everyone who ever lived,
Will take some time to sort.
Since the dawning of time,
Since the beginning of the Earth.
The names written in the Book of Life,
Have not lessened or gained girth.
God is in control,
This is not an empty statement.
Only the names of nonbelievers,

Will be lessened in abatement.

Salvation is a free gift,
It is very easy to receive.
Only ask Jesus to forgive you,
Then on Him believe.
Jesus is here with us,
His presence can be felt.
If only your hard, cold hearts,
You would allow to melt.
I know the Bible is true,
Jesus Himself is the Word.
Jesus said we are worth much more,
Than the value of any bird.
He sees every sparrow that falls,
Watches over all of His creation.
You see, the Father knows,
The answer to all equations.

If anyone who reads this,
Wishes to seek salvation.
Ask Jesus to forgive your sins,
Ask He who died for you to be your
representation.
Yes, claim the blood,

The blood of Jesus your Savior.
A tremendous weight will be lifted from you,
You might notice a change in your behavior.
This enormous weight,
That has been lifted off your shoulders,
Will not ever return,
As you continue to grow older.
The saints & angels in Heaven,
All will be rejoicing.
We might possibly hear them,
Were it not for our own cheers we'll be
voicing!
Oh, what a joyous day it is,
When another joins our number!
If you're alive, it's not too late,
To awaken from your slumber.
I know there are many of you,
Who still refuse to believe.
It's taken me three days to get this posted,
There's but one reason I can conceive.
Satan did not want you to read this,
He desires your soul in Hell.
I remained stubbornly persistent,
For this is my duty to tell.

Ode to Josie. 6-2-23

Ya'll gather 'round,
I'd like to tell you a story;
It's a beautiful story, about a beautiful girl,
That beautiful girl is my sister Joy.
Sometimes the story is happy,
And sometimes the story is sad;
But the story is always full of love—
Love and Hope, always Hope...
Grit, Truth, Endurance, and Drive...
The Drive to continue living,
When you really don't care if you live or die...
'Cause you lost the Apple of your eye.
It's tough to keep going,
When one you bore dies.
Dallas is still with us,
Yet we miss him every day;
I sense him always near me,

He's in my thoughts every day.

I remember long ago,
Long ago when we were kids;
Playing with a shoebox, a piece of twine,
bread, and a stick..
We'd try to catch a bird,
A bird we never caught.
I don't remember ever coming close,
To trapping a bird in the shoebox,
I do recall a day I was in the yard by the tree,
Joy told me to stand still because a snake was
behind me.
A little green garter snake,
A snake as harmless as a snake could be.
But when you're 3 & 4, or 4 & 5,
When you see a snake,
You want to flee!
Somewhere safe was Mom...
It was and forever will be.

In June each year...
On the day of June 19th;
Each year, a special day,
Special because it is Joy's BIRTHDAY!!!

Every year when we were kids,
Each year on June 19;
Joy would age and suddenly be...
Suddenly be, two years older than me.
As the years went by,
And time sure does fly,
It seemed Joy forgot that on her birthday,
Once again she would be two years older than me.
So being a good brother...
The good brother I strive to be;
It seemed my job to remind her,
Remind her I do,
This you can believe!
We always share a good laugh,
I love to see Joy smile...
That is when life's is best,
Joy's smile makes my life worthwhile.

In Autumn each year,
We'd get out and rake leaves,
Even asking our neighbors...
If we rake them, can we keep yours, please?
Then we'd take these leaves,
Home to add with ours.

We loved playing in our leaves,
We'd play in them for hours.
We'd play King of the Hill
Putting the leaves in one big pile.
We'd knock each other down,
I remember the laughter and smiles.
I don't recall a single frown,
For the leaves would cushion our landing,
They were always so soft,
The King was the last one standing.
That these were the best of days,
We would have never thought!
These memories are priceless,
They can't be stolen, sold, or bought!

As we entered high school,
Joy was there to cheer;
At football and basketball games,
Those were great and fun years!
We knew all the kids at school,
They liked us and we liked them too.
We partied a lot,
Partying was a lot of fun.
I overdid it at times,
Yet, I was the one.

I'd get so high...
I would not have a care.
I'd go to school high,
And get high while I was there;
It was normal for me,
While others didn't dare.
We all knew that life,
Wasn't always fair.
Joy was there for me,
Each time I'd done wrong;
She would take up for me...
At school or at home.
Chicken pox and mumps...
We had them together;
Those are the times,
I often remember.
Joy's always been,
My very best friend;
She will always be...
Right to the end!

Joy's always been special,
She has been all her life;
If I'd gotten to choose sisters,
I'd pick Joy and Trish and never think twice!

These two are a lot alike,
Yet different in their own ways;
I remember Mom telling Joy…
"Take your sister with you,
If you're going out to play…"
Joy would smile and obey…
Well, most times anyway.
For a while it seemed,
Each time Joy went somewhere,
Her shadow was with her…
Joy didn't seem to care.
Except for the time,
Joy was asked to stay all night;
Joy said she can't come,
It just isn't right.
They both had great dogs…
Trish had Bandit, Joy had Waylon;
They were always around,
They always were playin'.

One day a while back,
Joy and I were talking…
About the day I went away,
The Air Force was calling.
I thought I remembered that day,

That I went away so well;
Yet Joy's memory was better,
So this I must tell.
Joy looked at me and said,
"That Tuesday I was so sad."
This absolutely floored me,
As nothing before ever had.
Joy had remembered,
What day of the week I'd left;
This touched me deep in my soul,
So deep I could've wept.
There's no way I could've said,
"It was on a Tuesday I went away."
The fact that Joy remembered this,
Overwhelms me to this day.

We've been through both good and bad times,
More good than bad I hope;
Joy's so loving and caring,
She really is DOPE!
We've laughed and cried together,
We've been ecstatic and dismayed;
We've shared each day of my life,
I've never known any other way.
I can't imagine my life without her,

My elder, little Sis;
Each time I think of Joy,
My memories bring bliss.
Life without Joy would be empty,
As empty as Jesus' tomb;
I'm ever so thankful,
We came from the same womb.

My most frightening experience,
Happened when we were kids;
Dad was playing fast-pitch softball,
We were there to watch like we always did.
Joy and I wandered off through the woods,
We were wading down a creek,
We had no idea we were nearing,
A waterfall that was so steep.
Thank God for the fence,
It may have been a gate;
Either way it saved Joy,
From a sad, tragic fate.
See the creek disappeared,
It vanished from sight;
Straight down it plunged,
At least 70 feet, if I am right.
If you went over, you'd be a goner,

Of that I've no doubt;
Joy slipped on a rock,
She fell and almost found out.
Joy grabbed the fence,
It surely saved the day,
We never told anyone,
What happened that day.
In my mind's eye...
I can see it replay,
I knelt down on my knees,
And right there I prayed.
Thank You Lord for all You do,
And for never looking away,
But mostly Sweet Lord,
Thanks for saving Joy's life today!

I have so many memories,
They won't fit on any page;
My sister many thought was my twin,
Way back in the day.
My heart's filled with love for her,
Filled to the brim and overflowing;
I'd gladly give my life for hers,
Even without her knowing.
I told ya she was special,

Special, Joy truly is;
Yet she's more than just special,
My angelic older Sis.
I wish I could tell you,
Just what all Joy means to me;
I don't have the words,
If I did, it'd take all eternity.

That is the first time ever,
Something I wrote made me cry;
I Love You So Much Josie,
I don't even have to try!

A few things I failed to mention,
It would surely be a crime;
If I neglected to tell you,
Some things that just came to mind.
Back when I was 8 or 9,
Which would make Joy 9 or 10...or 10 or 11...
lol
We'd go visit MawMaw Fowler,
We were her piece of almost heaven;
It amazes me still,
How she'd show us our worth;
She'd save her money all year,

To take us to Camden Park each Fourth!
When we'd go see her,
In Chapmanville town;
We'd sing for MawMaw,
"Country Roads take me home."

There's a time I remember,
One time above all;
In Charleston
I spoke into the speaker,
The DJ heard it all.
I said, play Little Willie,
And Playground in My Mind.

The songs I'd requested,
Were the next two in line!
Remember, in Terri Stowers' basement,
Ya'll lifted me up using only two fingers,
Two fingers on each hand,
Sort of an Ouija board harbinger.
Chanting "Stiff as a Board & Light as a Feather."
Lifted me up over your heads..
Dropped me from the ceiling above,
The concrete floor stopped me dead.

I hope we're always close,
I know we will be;
There are no twins anywhere,
With a bond as tight as we!

Love Ya, Josie!
Geno

Trish

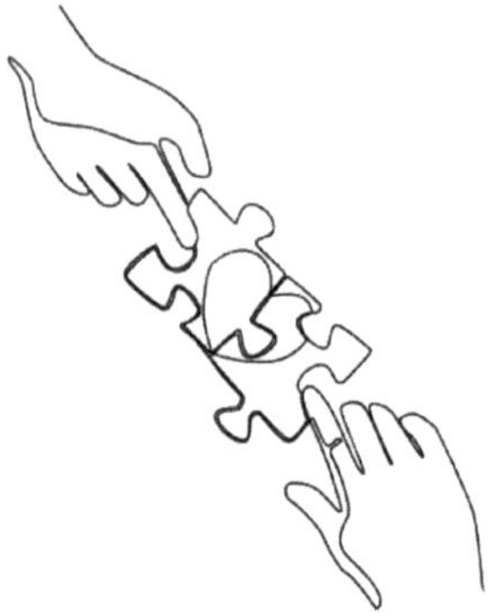

Trish, you were so many firsts for me,
Before you, I had no idea how babies came to be.
I knew you were in Mom's stomach,
Exactly how, I could not see.
Then after you began to crawl,
You really were a living doll,
I remember back when you began to walk,
I'm not sure if you were able to talk.
You'd stand by the coffee table or couch,
You were strong, your grip was no slouch,
We'd sit on the floor while you would linger,
You'd walk to us, holding onto our finger.
One day when I put my finger out you pushed it away,
Three times, and I wondered what's going on

today?
That day I saw your mental determination,
The look on your face was total
concentration.
Before I figured out what was going on,
You took three or four steps and fell into my
arms!
I was elated and proud as can be,
My little sister took her first steps to me!
I watched over you to keep you from harm,
You were cute with your curly hair, bursting
with charm,
I remember lying beside you while you had a
nap,
If your bottle fell away, I'd put it back in a
snap.
As you grew older you were great to have
around,
You'd do anything we asked... as Joy and I
soon found,
After a while you began telling us no,
We'd say, "We'll time you," and off you would
go!
Your dog Bandit, was your constant
companion,

You'd get so dark at the pool because of your complexion.
If I'd known then, I would've bought stock,
In Doritos and Oscar Mayer, it would've been a lock,
Nacho cheese & fried bologna each day for lunch,
So smart and pretty, we loved you a bunch.
We always have and we always will,
Just as sure as some pickles are made with dill,
I remember you and Lori, swimming in the pool,
You were so good at softball, volleyball too!
You always made good grades when you were in school,
You had it going on, yeah you were so cool
You went with Dad to a lot of Logan's basketball games,
Willie Akers had some great teams adding to his fame.
I used to skip school to go watch them with Dad,
A whole week in Morgantown, what great times we had.

I had some keg parties up at Ballard's river lot,
Remembering you and Chris...these things can't be bought,
MawMaw Fowler adored you so much, you almost took my spot,
But my spot as her favorite couldn't be got.
MawMaw & PawPaw sure loved you too,
You and Amy were ornery maybe even Laura Sue,
Dad always said we didn't know we had it made,
Truer words were never spoken—too bad life couldn't be delayed.
You were only eleven when I left for the Air Force,
To me, that's unbelievable, of course.
Looking back now it seems you should've been older,
We've had a lot of fun running shoulder-to-shoulder.
I remember a football game up in Morgantown,
We didn't make it in, we never saw a down,
That's not exactly true we watched the whole

game,
On TV at your friend's, we had a great time all the same.
We had so much fun I never wanted it to end,
Age has mellowed us some, I bet we'd still contend.
The first and only sibling younger than me,
You're my favorite little sister, I can say with complete honesty.
As we grow older it's easy to drift apart,
I'm glad we've always been close from the bottom of my heart.❤
I can't remember you ever making me too mad,
Neither can Joy—Mark's cornered the market on that.
Except for one time, about you I heard a rumor,
I heard someone was calling you Sooner,
That someone was Dad...Sooner was a girl in a movie,
For not being a hippy, at times Dad could be groovy.
I couldn't see then what I now see so clearly,
I'm so glad you came along...I LOVE YOU

Delta Dawn (revisited)

I've often wondered what became of Delta Dawn,
Where did she go...did she ever get picked up on?
Pining away can sure take a toll on your mind,
What became of Delta Dawn, I wondered time after time.
So I wrote this poem...I guess it could be a song,
She was a beauty that every guy hit on.
Was that her I saw passed out on someone's lawn?
Yeah, I've often wondered what became of Delta Dawn.

If you're asking about Dawn,
There's not a whole lot I can tell ya;
'Ceptin she came from down south,
From down around the Mississippi Delta;
Some folk say she married a rich man,
Some say he was her father;
They say he showed up one day,
She took him up on his offer.

Delta Dawn... where has your flower gone,
Was it a rose faded by days gone by?
What'd ya say...what was that you mumbled;
You shoved him down the stairs that time.
Then said he fell because he stumbled.

She's his widow now,
He's been deceased for quite a while;
Since the day he passed away,
No one around here has seen her smile.
May have been New Orleans,
That she hailed from;
She seems like a lost soul,
Walks around like she's still looking for
someone.

Delta Dawn, won't you tell us,
Just where do you hail from;
Was it New Orleans,
Or another town under the sun.
Was it just one little shove,
When the man you loved tumbled;
Did he suffer afore he died,
Some say he may have grumbled.

Some say she'd made a stop along the way,
In Brownsville, Tennessee if you'd believe what they say;
That's where she met a man who had a guitar in his hand,
Said he was gonna be a star in his very own rock & roll band.

She went to see his band play,
Discovered there was truth in what he'd said;
She got swept away when she heard him play,
That very night she wound up in his bed.
Then came the day he went on the road,
Promised he'd send for her before too long;
Now she walks around town with an old

suitcase in her hand,
The very one they sang about...in that other song.

Delta Dawn, where have your flowers gone,
Did they get blown away... like a tumbleweed in the wind;
Whatever happened to your man... in that rock & roll band,
Do ya reckon we'll ever see that man again?
Now Dawn, don't get me wrong...
I just made up this silly song,
I truly hope you find your happiness one of these days;
You're so sweet and kind...it's a shame you've lost your mind,
Some say you can still hear your man and his guitar play.

For Stephen King

Word sure does get around,
Like bad news in a small town;
Did you hear about Pennywise the clown?
We all float when the sun goes down.

Have you ever seen a storm sewer full of rain?
Have you ever been to any small town in
Maine?
Have you ever read a story written by the
great Stephen King?
If you ever got the opportunity to meet him,
what would you bring?

A copy of *The Stand* to get autographed?
Or some real funny jokes, to make him laugh?
Would you bring an instrument, and ask to
join his band?

Would you perhaps tell him you're his
number one fan?

Ya reckon that would make him nervous?
Would you watch his reaction with a big grin?
I'd take some good pot and fishing poles,
We'd get real high, relax, and each have a new
friend.

Ringo

The best birthday gift,
That I ever received;
Is actually two,
Would you believe three?
My two sisters took me,
To Charleston to see Ringo,
It was a helluva show,
Except they didn't have a banjo.
Ringo is so special,
If ever you get the chance,
GO AND SEE HIM!
This great man's aura,
Filled up the whole Colosseum!
Ringo left the stage,
While Edgar played Frankenstein;
His aura left a void,
The people who were there,
All know I'm not lyin'!!

On John Lennon's birthday no less,
A wonderful way to celebrate,
With one of John's bandmates;
Seeing a Beatle on stage,
It truly was great!

I was at my buddy's apartment the next day,
Looking at Nolan Ryan baseball cards.
Mike slipped me my present,
I'd never been so shocked.
I said, "This looks like John Lennon."
"It's autographed," he said, then, "Happy
Birthday!"
Don't know if I'll ever recover,
It totally blew me away!
Two gifts, both priceless,
Gifts I can never repay.
To thank them properly,
I don't have the words to say.
I just thought of something,
That I've neglected to mention;
A gift that's also priceless,
Of that, there's no question.
This gift was a jacket,
From a Facebook friend of mine;

Oh Boy! Let me tell ya,
It was top-of-the-line.
It suits me to a tee,
Never saw a jacket so fine;
On it, there's a collage of photos,
Of "Handsome Johnny" Prine!

These three ambassadors of LOVE,
John, Ringo, and John;
Carried the olive branch of peace,
Brother Ringo carries it on.
It seems we're always at war,
Had wars for way too long;
Let's all "Give Peace a Chance,"
Like Lennon sang in his song!
I believe we could do this,
We won't know if we don't try;

We all let these wars start,
I can't "IMAGINE" why;
They want what we have,
We want what they have,
We want what they've got,
Why not negotiate a deal?
It'd beat the hell outta being shot!

Ravenswood

Sitting on Kracker Korner,
A real place in my hometown;
I watch the children play,
On my city's new playground.
Uncle Kracker played here last year,
People came from miles around;
Of course, my favorite time to visit here,
Is when the sun goes down.

Ravenswoodites go inside,
When the nighttime falls;
They roll up the sidewalks,
To us, "Deadwood" it was called.
Some things never change,
In this small Ohio River town;
Not saying we've not made progress,
Mayor Miller's vision is profound.

A new playground in City Park,
Isn't the only project on the table;
Astroturf on Flinn Field,
Football's an old Ravenswood staple.
Another noteworthy project,
Happening around town;
Across from Riverfront Park,
A floating boat dock & campground.

Back here at Kracker Korner,
Is now a four-way stop;
Commit that to memory,
Else you just might meet a cop.
When the potrooms shut down,
Over at the aluminum plant;
I thought our town might be over,
But now I must recant.

My town is full of great people,
Resilient and daring;
Other places I've lived,
The people seem uncaring.
Growing up in Ravenswood,
Felt like we were all related;

If not brothers & sisters,
Distant cousins, not obligated.

Everyone was family,
We all knew each other;
We had more than two parents,
We had lots of fathers and mothers.
All of our friend's parents,
Genuinely cared for our well-being;
Made it hard sneaking around,
Adult eyes were all-seeing.

These memories come flooding back,
As I sit here on Kracker Korner;
Looking at the ballfields, library, & Farmers Bank,
All are welcome here...no one is a foreigner.
Home of the friendliest people,
Friendly but competitive;
We'll always compete,
Though you might hear some expletives.

Located at the Big Bend,
Of the Ohio River;
Given any situation,

Ravenswood always delivers.
I take pride in my hometown,
Even though pride is a sin;
If ya get a chance to visit,
You're guaranteed to be welcomed in.

Money

Money might not buy happiness,
I guess it can rent a good time;
Money's a concept of man,
Making your own is looked upon as a crime.
Hey, you over there,
Covered in dirt and grime;
I'll pay you a penny a day,
If you toil in these fields of mine.
Workers have been paid a pittance,
If they're even paid at all;
Some work for room and board,
I believe slavery's what that's called.
I own the land and you do the work,
How's an 80-20 split sound?
I'll even throw in a bonus,
When you die I'll bury you in my ground.
Who could refuse that offer?
He made me an offer I couldn't refuse;
I cannot ever refuse his orders,
I'm forever paying my dues.
Should I ever disobey him,
He might sell off my son or daughter;
If I work real hard and do a good job,

He might even provide some cool water.

Get out there in the noon-day sun,
While I sit over here in the shade;
Workers have it better now,
But sadly unions are fading away.
I don't mean to compare now to slavery,
I'm certain the slaves would trade places;
Unions need to come back stronger,
Regain what these last 40 years have erased.
This didn't happen at once,
The oppression slowly trickled down;
Exactly how they said money would,
The day Reaganomics rode into town.
Capital is the result of labor,
Without labor nothing gets made;
Think about this, I ask you,
What good is a brick that's not laid?
They claim job creation's a favor,
Is a job not filled, a job?
Workers deserve a bigger slice of the pie,
At 60-40 we'd still be getting robbed.
Corporation owners these days are so greedy,
Greed is the love of money;
The love of money is the root of all evil,

That's why rich men in heaven won't be many.

True Victory

When I imagine victory, the image that
appears in my mind,
Dale Earnhardt at Daytona shaking hands all
down the pit road line;
1998 it was...he had come so darn close so
many times,
He hit a seagull on the backstretch while
leading on the last lap,
Another year he ran out of gas while leading
the white flag lap!
In '98 the Goodwrench Chevrolet drove to
victory lane,
We did it! We did it! We did it! We heard him
so plain!
The Daytona 500...it is the Super Bowl of
racing,
Once disgusted he guessed he wasn't supposed
to win the damn thing!
A true champion drove the wheels off that
black number three that day,
That each man on pit road shook his hand put
his greatness on display;
That was so dramatic because it had never

happened before,
An awesome tribute to the man they called the Intimidator!
The Man in Black was smiling...high fives were going 'round and 'round,
Look as close and hard as you like, you weren't going to find a frown;
They all knew how bad he wanted it...all the hard work he'd put in,
It surely was a pleasure to see him with that devilish grin.
A short three years later, the final lap once again held his fate,
It was the day when the greatest ever...Dale Earnhardt became late;
A tragic day, emotions were raw, at "The Great American Race,"
The wings of victory flew Dale away...to race some other place.
The Winston Cup Championships he won in all numbered seven,
The greatest victory of all awaits believers in heaven;
I know there are many who won't accept Lord Jesus as their Savior,

Some who wouldn't see heaven were it based
on our behavior;
I now see the mistake I made when first I
pictured victory,
The greatest victory man ever saw was won at
Calvary!

9 789363 305304

Printed by Libri Plureos GmbH in Hamburg, Germany